D0307159

GOOD HOUSEKEEPING

SUMMER COOKING

Say goodbye to boring salads when you open up this book. Turn the pages and see how to add interest and zest to the fabulous ingredients of summer—there is no better time of the year for creating wonderful food for family and friends. The choice of fresh, seasonal ingredients is virtually limitless in summertime: crisp and crunchy vegetables, plus the most colourful array of soft fruits just waiting for eating. With this book to hand, you'll never be stuck for eating ideas all the summer long.

With the compliments of

COOKERY NOTES

Follow either metric or imperial measures for the recipes in this book as they are not interchangeable. Sets of spoon measures are available in both metric and imperial size to give accurate measurement of small quantities. All spoon measures are level unless otherwise stated. When measuring milk we have used the exact conversion of 568 ml (1 pint).
* Size 2 eggs should be used except when otherwise stated.
† Granulated sugar is used unless otherwise stated.
● Plain flour is used unless otherwise stated.

OVEN TEMPERATURE CHART

°C	°F	Gas mark
110	225	$\frac{1}{4}$
130	250	$\frac{1}{2}$
140	275	1
150	300	2
170	325	3
180	350	4
190	375	5
200	400	6
220	425	7
230	450	8
240	475	9

KEY TO SYMBOLS

$\boxed{1.00^*}$ Indicates minimum preparation and cooking times in hours and minutes. They do not include prepared items in the list of ingredients; calculated times apply only to the method. An asterisk * indicates extra time should be allowed, so check the note below symbols.

⌂ Chef's hats indicate degree of difficulty of a recipe: no hat means it is straightforward; one hat slightly more complicated; two hats indicates that it is for more advanced cooks.

£ Indicates a recipe which is good value for money; £ £ indicates an expensive recipe. No £ sign indicates an inexpensive recipe.

✳ Indicates that a recipe will freeze. If there is no symbol, the recipe is unsuitable for freezing. An asterisk * indicates special freezer instructions so check the note immediately below the symbols.

$\boxed{309 \text{ cals}}$ Indicates calories per serving, including any suggestions (e.g. cream, to serve) given in the ingredients.

METRIC CONVERSION SCALE

	LIQUID			SOLID	
Imperial	Exact conversion	Recommended ml	Imperial	Exact conversion	Recommended g
$\frac{1}{4}$ pint	142 ml	150 ml	1 oz	28.35 g	25 g
$\frac{1}{2}$ pint	284 ml	300 ml	2 oz	56.7 g	50 g
1 pint	568 ml	600 ml	4 oz	113.4 g	100 g
$1\frac{1}{2}$ pints	851 ml	900 ml	8 oz	226.8 g	225 g
$1\frac{3}{4}$ pints	992 ml	1 litre	12 oz	340.2 g	350 g
For quantities of $1\frac{3}{4}$ pints and over, litres and fractions of a litre have been used.			14 oz	397.0 g	400 g
			16 oz (1 lb)	453.6 g	450 g
			1 kilogram (kg) equals 2.2 lb.		

Illustrated on the cover: Strawberries with Raspberry Sauce (page 56)

GOOD HOUSEKEEPING

SUMMER COOKING

Contents

SOUPS AND STARTERS	4
MAIN COURSES	16
SALADS	34
DESSERTS	40
INDEX	62

GAZPACHO

0.30* £ ❄	154 cals

* plus 2 hours chilling

Serves 4

100 g (4 oz) green pepper

1 medium cucumber

450 g (1 lb) fully ripened tomatoes

50–100 g (2–4 oz) onions, skinned

1 garlic clove, skinned

45 ml (3 tbsp) vegetable oil

45 ml (3 tbsp) white wine vinegar

425-g (15-oz) can tomato juice

30 ml (2 tbsp) tomato purée

1.25 ml ($\frac{1}{4}$ tsp) salt

green pepper, ice cubes and croûtons, to serve

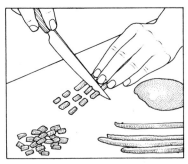

1 Remove the core and seeds from the green pepper and chop roughly with the cucumber, tomatoes, onion and garlic.

2 Mix the ingredients together in a bowl. Place in a blender or food processor in small portions and blend to form a smooth purée. Chill for 2 hours.

3 To serve. Core and seed the green pepper; dice very finely. Pour purée into bowl and add a few ice cubes. Serve garnished with diced pepper and croûtons.

ICED COURGETTE SOUP

0.40*	✳*	260 cals

* plus cooling and overnight chilling;
freeze at the end of step 3

Serves 4

50 g (2 oz) butter or margarine

450 g (1 lb) courgettes, trimmed
and chopped

1 medium potato, peeled and diced

750 ml ($1\frac{1}{4}$ pints) vegetable stock or
water

5 ml (1 tsp) chopped fresh basil or
2.5 ml ($\frac{1}{2}$ tsp) dried basil

salt and freshly ground pepper

100 g (4 oz) ripe Blue Brie

sliced courgette, to serve (optional)

1 Melt the butter or margarine
in a large heavy-based
saucepan. Add the courgettes and
potato, cover the pan and fry
gently for about 10 minutes until
softened, shaking frequently.

2 Add the stock or water with
the basil and seasoning to
taste. Bring to the boil, stirring,
then lower the heat and simmer
for 20 minutes until the vegetables
are tender.

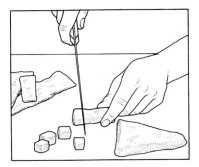

3 Remove the rind from the Brie
and chop the cheese into small
dice. Put into a blender or food
processor, then pour in the soup.
Blend until smooth, then turn into
a bowl, cover and leave until cold.
Chill in the refrigerator overnight.

4 Whisk the soup vigorously to
ensure an even consistency,
then taste and adjust seasoning.
Pour into a chilled soup tureen or
individual bowls and float the
courgette slices on the top if liked.

ICED TOMATO AND HERB SOUP

| 0.20* f ✳ | 133 cals |

* plus 2 hours chilling

Serves 4

450 g (1 lb) ripe tomatoes

1 small onion, skinned and sliced

20 ml (4 tsp) tomato purée

411 g ($14\frac{1}{2}$ oz) can chicken
  consommé

30 ml (2 tbsp) chopped fresh herbs
  e.g. basil, coriander, parsley

salt and freshly ground pepper

25 g (1 oz) fresh white
  breadcrumbs

150 ml ($\frac{1}{4}$ pint) soured cream

fresh basil leaves, to garnish

1 Roughly chop the tomatoes
and process them with the
onion, tomato purée, consommé
and herbs until smooth.

2 Rub the tomato mixture
through a nylon sieve into a
saucepan. Heat gently to remove
the frothy texture, then add plenty
of salt and pepper.

3 Pour the soup into a large
serving bowl and stir in the
breadcrumbs. Chill in the
refrigerator for at least 2 hours.

4 Stir the soured cream until
smooth, then swirl in. Float
the fresh basil leaves on top.

ASPARAGUS MOUSSES

$\boxed{1.45}$ ⊟ £ £ $\boxed{235 \text{ cals}}$

Serves 6

700 g (1½ lb) fresh asparagus

50 g (2 oz) butter

1 medium onion, skinned and finely chopped

30 ml (2 tbsp) lemon juice

150 ml (¼ pint) double cream

3 egg yolks

salt and freshly ground pepper

1 egg white

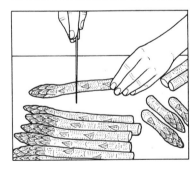

1 Cut the heads off the asparagus to a length of about 4 cm (1½ inches) and reserve. Slice the stalks into 1 cm (½ inch) lengths, discarding any particularly tough root ends.

2 Melt the butter in a medium saucepan. Add the asparagus stalks, onion and lemon juice, then pour in 200 ml (7 fl oz) water. Cover tightly and cook gently for about 30 minutes, or until the asparagus is tender.

3 Drain the asparagus well, then put in a blender or food processor with the cream. Work until almost smooth.

4 Rub the purée through a nylon sieve into a bowl to remove any stringy particles. Beat in the egg yolks with salt and pepper to taste. Whisk the egg white until stiff and fold into the asparagus mixture.

5 Spoon the asparagus mixture into six 150 ml (¼ pint) ramekins, then stand the dishes in a roasting tin. Pour in enough hot water to come half way up the sides of the ramekins.

6 Bake the mousses in the oven at 170°C (325°F) mark 3 for 40–45 minutes or until the centres are just firm to the touch.

7 Ten minutes before the end of the cooking time, steam the asparagus heads for 5–10 minutes until tender. Serve the mousses immediately, topped with the asparagus heads.

TOMATO ICE WITH VEGETABLE JULIENNE

0.45^* ⬡ £ ✳ 175–263 cals

* plus 6 hours freezing and 30 minutes softening

Serves 4–6

8 very ripe tomatoes

10 ml (2 tsp) gelatine

30 ml (2 tbsp) tomato purée

30 ml (2 tbsp) lemon juice or juice of $\frac{1}{2}$ lemon

a few drops of Tabasco

salt and freshly ground pepper

1 egg white (optional)

30 ml (2 tbsp) chopped fresh basil leaves (optional)

2 small leeks

2 medium carrots, peeled

2 medium courgettes

150 ml ($\frac{1}{4}$ pint) Vinaigrette

fresh basil leaves, to garnish (optional)

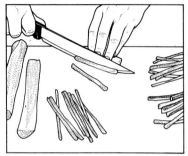

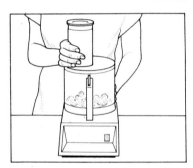

1 Put the tomatoes in a blender or food processor and work until smooth. Press the tomato pulp through a sieve into a bowl to remove the seeds and skin.

2 Put 45 ml (3 tbsp) very hot water in a small bowl and sprinkle in the gelatine. Stir briskly until dissolved, then leave to cool slightly.

3 Add the tomato purée to the tomato pulp with the lemon juice, Tabasco and salt and pepper to taste. Mix thoroughly.

4 Stir in the gelatine and chopped basil leaves (if using). Pour into a chilled shallow freezer container and freeze for about 2 hours until mushy.

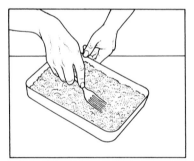

5 Remove the container from the freezer and beat the mixture with a fork to break down any ice crystals. Return to the freezer and freeze for a further 4 hours. (If a creamier texture is desired, whisk the egg white until stiff, fold into the beaten mixture and return to the freezer. Freeze as before.)

6 Meanwhile, wash the leeks thoroughly and cut into fine julienne strips of equal length. Cut the carrots and courgettes into julienne strips of the same size.

7 Bring a large pan of water to the boil and add the leeks. Blanch for 1 minute, then remove with a slotted spoon and drain on absorbent kitchen paper. Blanch the carrots in the same water for about 4 minutes, remove and drain well. Similarly, blanch the courgettes for 2 minutes and then drain them well.

8 Put the julienne of vegetables in a bowl, add the vinaigrette and salt and pepper to taste and toss gently to mix. Cover and chill in the refrigerator until required.

9 To serve, allow the tomato ice to soften in the refrigerator for 30 minutes. Arrange small scoops of tomato ice on chilled individual side plates with a 'nest' of julienne vegetables. Garnish with fresh basil sprigs, if using.

HUMMUS
(MIDDLE EASTERN CHICK PEA AND TAHINI DIP)

1.20*	£	✳*	277–416 cals

* plus overnight soaking and a few hours chilling; freeze without the garnish

Serves 4–6

175 g (6 oz) chick peas, soaked in cold water overnight

about 150 ml ($\frac{1}{4}$ pint) lemon juice

150 ml ($\frac{1}{4}$ pint) tahini paste

3 garlic cloves, skinned and crushed

salt

30 ml (2 tbsp) olive oil

5 ml (1 tsp) paprika

crudités, to serve (see box)

1 Drain the soaked chick peas and rinse well under cold running water. Put the chick peas in a large saucepan and cover with plenty of cold water.

2 Bring slowly to the boil, then skim off any scum with a slotted spoon. Half cover the pan with a lid and simmer gently for about 1 hour, until the chick peas are very tender.

3 Drain the chick peas, reserving 60 ml (4 tbsp) of the cooking liquid. Set a few whole chick peas aside for the garnish, then put the remainder in a blender or food processor. Add the reserved cooking liquid and half of the lemon juice and work to a smooth purée.

4 Add the tahini paste, garlic and 5 ml (1 tsp) salt and work again. Taste and add more lemon juice until the dip is to your liking, then blend in 30 ml (2 tbsp) hot water.

5 Turn into a serving bowl and cover with cling film. Chill in the refrigerator until serving time. Before serving, mix the oil with the paprika and drizzle over the Hummus. Arrange the reserved whole chick peas on top.

PAPA GHANOOYE
(ARABIC AUBERGINE DIP)

0.50*	£	✳*	322–483 cals

* plus a few hours chilling; freeze without the garnish

Serves 4–6

2 large aubergines

salt

2–3 garlic cloves, skinned and roughly chopped

10 ml (2 tsp) cumin seeds

100 ml (4 fl oz) olive oil

150 ml ($\frac{1}{4}$ pint) tahini paste

about 100 ml (4 fl oz) lemon juice

thin tomato slices, to garnish

crudités, to serve (see box)

1 Slice the aubergines, then place in a colander, sprinkling each layer with salt. Cover with a plate, put heavy weights on top and leave to dégorge for 30 minutes.

2 Meanwhile, crush the garlic and cumin seeds with a pestle and mortar. Add 5 ml (1 tsp) salt and mix well.

3 Rinse the aubergines under cold running water, then pat dry with absorbent kitchen paper. Heat the oil in a large, heavy-based frying pan until very hot. Add the aubergine slices in batches and fry until golden on both sides, turning once. Remove from the pan with a slotted spoon and drain again on kitchen paper.

4 Put the aubergine slices in a blender or food processor with the garlic mixture, the tahini paste and about two-thirds of the lemon juice. Work to a smooth purée, then taste and add more lemon juice and salt if liked.

5 Turn into a serving bowl, cover with cling film and chill in the refrigerator until serving time. Serve chilled, garnished with tomato slices.

SKORDALIA
(GREEK GARLIC DIP)

0.30*	£	381–572 cals

* plus a few hours chilling

Serves 4–6

75 g (3 oz) crustless white bread

60 ml (4 tbsp) milk

6 garlic cloves

250 ml (8 fl oz) olive oil

about 50 ml (2 fl oz) lemon juice

salt and freshly ground pepper

black olives and finely chopped parsley, to garnish

crudités, to serve (see box)

1 Tear the bread into small pieces into a bowl. Add the milk, mix and soak for 5 minutes.

2 Skin the cloves of garlic, chop roughly, then crush with a pestle and mortar.

3 Squeeze the bread with your fingers, then mix with the crushed garlic. Add the olive oil a drop at a time to form a paste.

4 When the mixture thickens, add a few drops of lemon juice, then continue with the olive oil. Add more lemon juice and salt and pepper. Turn into a bowl and cover with cling film. Chill in the refrigerator and garnish with olives and parsley before serving.

VEGETABLE DIPS

Dips make good starters for informal supper parties, or to serve at a drinks party. Crudités (raw vegetables) are ideal for dipping and dunking. To serve 4–6 people: 4 carrots, peeled and cut into thin sticks, 1 small cauliflower, divided into florets, 4–6 celery sticks, halved, $\frac{1}{2}$ cucumber, seeds removed and cut into sticks, 1 red and 1 green pepper, cored seeded and sliced, 1 bunch of radishes, trimmed. Fingers of hot pitta bread can also be served.

AVOCADO WITH PRAWNS AND SMOKED SALMON

| 0.25 | £ £ | 439 cals |

Serves 4

60 ml (4 tbsp) mayonnaise

60 ml (4 tbsp) soured cream or natural yogurt

30 ml (2 tbsp) snipped chives

10 ml (2 tsp) lemon juice

a few drops of Tabasco sauce

salt and freshly ground pepper

100 g (4 oz) smoked salmon

100 g (4 oz) peeled prawns, defrosted and thoroughly dried if frozen

2 ripe avocados

lemon wedges and 4 unpeeled prawns (optional), to garnish

1 Make the dressing. Put the mayonnaise in a bowl with the soured cream or yogurt, chives, lemon juice and Tabasco sauce to taste. Add plenty of salt and pepper, then whisk vigorously with a fork to combine all the ingredients together.

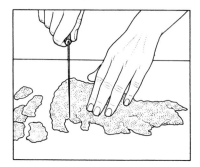

2 Cut the smoked salmon into bite-sized pieces. Chop the prawns roughly. Add to the dressing and fold gently to mix.

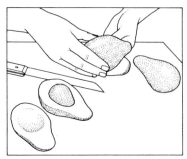

3 Just before serving, halve and stone the avocados. Scoop out the flesh and chop up small.

4 Fold the avocado into the fish mixture. Spoon into the avocado shells, garnish and serve immediately.

PRAWN AND DILL TARTLETS

| 1.00 | 🍲 | £ £ | ✳ | 462 cals |

Makes 6

75 g (3 oz) butter

25 g (1 oz) blended white vegetable fat

175 g (6 oz) plain flour

45 ml (3 tbsp) water

50 g (2 oz) spring onions, washed and finely chopped

2 egg yolks

200 ml (7 fl oz) double cream

2.5 ml ($\frac{1}{2}$ tsp) chopped fresh dill or 1.25 ml ($\frac{1}{4}$ tsp) dried

salt and freshly ground pepper

36 fresh prawns, peeled

6 unshelled prawns, to garnish

1 Make the pastry. Rub the fats into the flour and bind to a firm dough with the water. Knead lightly until just smooth. Chill in the refrigerator for 15 minutes.

2 Roll out the pastry thinly and use to line six individual fluted flan dishes. Bake the pastry 'blind' for 15 minutes until just set and beginning to colour.

3 Divide onions between flan dishes. Make custard mixture. Mix egg yolks, cream, dill and seasoning together and pour into the cases to fill two-thirds deep.

4 Arrange the prawns in the custard mixture, and bake in the oven at 170°C (325°F) mark 3 for 20 minutes until set. Garnish and serve warm, not hot.

13

SALADE TIÈDE AUX LARDONS

| 0.20 | £ | 526 cals |

Serves 4

135 ml (9 tbsp) olive oil

30 ml (2 tbsp) wine vinegar

2 garlic cloves, skinned and crushed

5 ml (1 tsp) French mustard

salt and freshly ground pepper

8 streaky bacon rashers, rinded

4 thick slices of white bread, crusts removed

30 ml (2 tbsp) single or double cream

1 small head of curly endive, leaves separated

1 Put 90 ml (6 tbsp) of the oil in a large salad bowl with the wine vinegar, garlic, mustard and salt and pepper to taste. Whisk with a fork until thick.

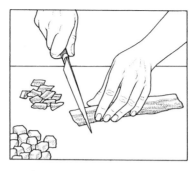

2 Cut the bacon and bread into small dice. Heat the remaining oil in a frying pan, add the bacon and bread and fry over brisk heat until crisp and golden brown on all sides. Remove with a slotted spoon and drain on absorbent kitchen paper.

3 Stir the cream into the dressing, then add the endive and warm bacon and croûtons. Toss quickly to combine and serve immediately.

DEEP-FRIED CAMEMBERT

$0.30*$ 680 cals

* plus 30 minutes chilling

Serves 4

8 individual portions of ripe
    Camembert

15 ml (1 tbsp) plain flour

salt and freshly ground pepper

1 egg, size 2

50 g (2 oz) dried breadcrumbs

25 g (1 oz) blanched almonds, very
    finely chopped

vegetable oil, for deep frying

cranberry or redcurrant jelly,
    to serve

4 Heat the oil in a deep-fat frier to 190°C (375°F). Deep fry the Camembert for about 4 minutes, turning to ensure even browning. Remove from the oil with a slotted spoon and drain on absorbent kitchen paper. Serve hot, with the cranberry or redcurrant jelly handed separately, for dipping.

DEEP-FRIED CAMEMBERT

The appeal of this delicious starter is the way in which the ripe Camembert cheese oozes out of its crisp coating when cut. Make sure the cheese is just ripe before coating, then keep it well chilled right up to the moment of deep-frying. If the cheese is allowed to stand at room temperature, it will become over-ripe and ooze out of the coating during frying.

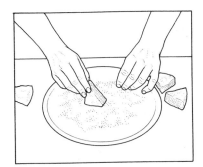

1 Coat the portions of Camembert in the flour seasoned with salt and pepper.

2 Beat the egg in a shallow dish, add the Camembert and turn to coat in the egg.

3 Mix the breadcrumbs and almonds together and coat the Camembert with it. Repeat with more egg, breadcrumbs and almonds to make a second coating. Freeze or chill for 30 minutes.

15

COLD BEEF IN SOURED CREAM

| 0.30* | £ £ | 318 cals |

* plus 2–3 hours chilling

Serves 6

1 large onion, skinned

350 g (12 oz) button mushrooms

700 g ($1\frac{1}{2}$ lb) lean rump steak in a thin slice

45 ml (3 tbsp) vegetable oil

salt and freshly ground pepper

7.5 ml ($1\frac{1}{2}$ tsp) Dijon mustard

7.5 ml ($1\frac{1}{2}$ tsp) chopped fresh thyme or 5 ml (1 tsp) dried

1 large green eating apple

284 ml (10 fl oz) soured cream

15 ml (1 tbsp) lemon juice

crisp lettuce and freshly toasted French bread, to serve

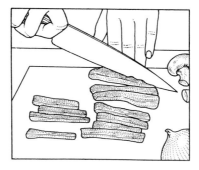

1 Using a sharp knife, finely chop the onion and finely slice the mushrooms. Slice the rump steak into thin strips.

2 Heat the oil in a large frying pan. Quickly brown the steak in a shallow layer, turning occasionally. Don't crowd the pan; cook the meat in two batches if necessary. The beef should remain pink in the centre.

3 Transfer the meat to a bowl using a slotted spoon. Season with salt and pepper.

4 Reheat the fat remaining in the pan. Fry the onion for 5 minutes until golden brown. Add the mushrooms, mustard and thyme. Cook over high heat for 1 minute. Add to beef; allow to cool; refrigerate for 2–3 hours.

5 Quarter and core the apple; slice thinly. Combine with the soured cream and lemon juice.

6 Line a shallow dish with lettuce. Combine the beef and apple mixtures and season. Pile into the centre of the lettuce. Serve with toasted French bread.

BEEF AND OLIVE SALAD

1.40* £ 341 cals

* plus about 2 hours cooling and
30 minutes chilling

Serves 4

450 g (1 lb) rolled lean brisket

1 bay leaf

6 peppercorns

1 large bunch of spring onions

12 black olives

450 g (1 lb) French beans

salt and freshly ground pepper

45 ml (3 tbsp) soy sauce

20 ml (4 tsp) lemon juice

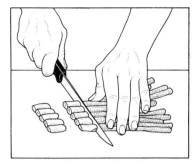

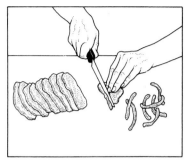

1 Put the beef, bay leaf and peppercorns in a small saucepan. Add enough water to cover. Bring to the boil, cover and simmer gently for about 1 hour or until the meat is tender. Leave to cool in the cooking liquid for about 2 hours.

2 Slice the spring onions diagonally into thick pieces. Quarter and stone the olives. Trim and halve the French beans. Cook the beans in boiling salted water for 5–10 minutes until just tender. Drain well, rinse under cold water and drain again thoroughly.

3 Drain the beef and trim off the fat. Slice thinly and cut into 4 cm ($1\frac{1}{2}$ inch) long shreds.

4 Put the beef in a bowl, add the spring onions, olives, beans, soy sauce and lemon juice. Toss well together, then season with pepper. (The soy sauce should provide sufficient salt.) Cover and chill in the refrigerator for about 30 minutes before serving.

——— VARIATION ———

Slice the beef into about 12 thin slices. Finely chop **20 stoned black olives** and mix with **1 crushed garlic clove** and **45 ml (3 tbsp) olive oil**. Spread the olive mixture thinly and evenly over both sides of each slice of beef. Roll up each slice loosely from the shortest end and arrange on a flat serving dish. Cover and chill in the refrigerator. Trim and thinly slice **1 large bunch of radishes**; skin and thinly slice **1 small onion**. Mix in a bowl with **15 ml (1 tbsp) olive oil**. Spoon the radish and onion mixture around the beef rolls.

FILLET STEAK EN CROÛTE WITH MUSHROOMS

1.30 ☐ ☐£ £✳* 763 cals

* freeze at end of step 9

Serves 8

350 g (12 oz) medium flat
 mushrooms

50 g (2 oz) butter or margarine

1 medium onion, skinned and
 finely chopped

100 g (4 oz) fresh breadcrumbs

2.5 ml ($\frac{1}{2}$ tsp) chopped fresh thyme
 or 1.25 ml ($\frac{1}{4}$ tsp) dried

salt and freshly ground pepper

1.4 kg (3 lb) fillet of beef, trimmed
 of all fat and gristle

two 368 g (13 oz) packets frozen
 puff pastry, thawed

1 egg, separated

parsley sprigs, to garnish

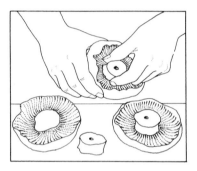

1 Remove the stems from 8
mushrooms and reserve the
caps. Chop the stems and the
remaining mushrooms finely.

2 Melt the butter in a large
frying pan, add the chopped
mushrooms and onion and cook
gently for about 10 minutes until
the onion is soft but not coloured.

3 Stir in the breadcrumbs and
thyme and season with salt and
pepper. Mix well and remove from
the heat.

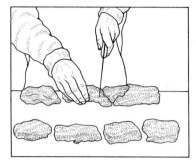

4 Cut the meat in half
lengthways, then slice each
half crossways into 4 equal pieces.
Dry the pieces of meat with
absorbent kitchen paper.

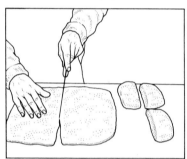

5 Cut each piece of pastry in
half. Roll out 1 piece to a
35.5 × 28 cm (14 × 11 inch)
rectangle, then cut in half. Roll
each half to 25.5 × 16 cm (10 × 6$\frac{1}{2}$
inches). Repeat with the remaining
pieces of pastry to make 8
rectangles altogether.

6 Put 60 ml (4 tbsp) of the
mushroom mixture in the
middle of 1 pastry rectangle. Place
a piece of beef on top and sprinkle
it with salt.

7 Top the beef with a whole
mushroom cap. Beat the egg
white with 10 ml (2 tsp) water and
brush this along the edges of the
pastry rectangle.

8 Fold the pastry over the meat
and mushroom, overlapping
the edges. Press lightly to seal.
Place seam-side down on a baking
sheet. Prepare the remaining
parcels in the same way.

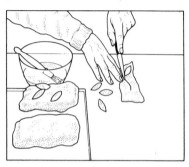

9 Roll out the pastry trimmings
and cut out decorative shapes.
Brush 1 side with the egg white
mixture and stick on to the pastry
parcels.

10 Chill the parcels in the
refrigerator until you are
ready to cook. Beat the egg yolk
with 10 ml (2 tsp) water and brush
this glaze over the pastry. Bake in
the oven at 200°C (400°F) mark 6,
allowing 25 minutes for rare beef
or 27 minutes for medium-cooked
beef. Transfer the parcels to a
large warmed serving dish or
individual plates. Serve
immediately garnished with the
parsley sprigs.

LAMB NOISETTES IN PORT AND REDCURRANT SAUCE

| 1.15 | £ £ ✳ | 527 cals |

Serves 2

4 lamb noisettes

plain flour, for coating

25 g (1 oz) butter

15 ml (1 tbsp) vegetable oil

1 small onion, skinned and finely chopped

1 garlic clove, skinned and crushed

60 ml (4 tbsp) ruby port

300 ml ($\frac{1}{2}$ pint) chicken stock

1 bay leaf

salt and freshly ground pepper

30 ml (2 tbsp) redcurrant jelly

fresh bay leaves, to garnish (optional)

1 Lightly coat the lamb noisettes with flour. Heat the butter and oil in a small flameproof casserole. Add the noisettes and brown quickly on both sides. Remove from the casserole with a slotted spoon and set aside.

2 Add the onion and garlic to the casserole and fry for about 5 minutes until golden. Stir in the port, stock and bay leaf. Season well with salt and pepper.

3 Replace the noisettes and bring to the boil, then cover and simmer gently for about 40 minutes until tender, turning the meat once during this time.

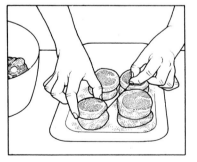

4 Lift the noisettes out of the sauce and remove the string. Place the noisettes on a warmed serving dish and keep hot.

5 Add the redcurrant jelly to the liquid in the casserole and boil rapidly for 5–10 minutes to reduce the sauce to about 150 ml ($\frac{1}{4}$ pint). Taste and adjust seasoning, remove the bay leaf, then pour the sauce over the noisettes. Serve immediately, garnished with fresh bay leaves, if liked.

20

LAMB WITH CUCUMBER AND MINT STUFFING

| 1.30 | £ £ ✳ | 695 cals |

Serves 4

$\frac{1}{2}$ cucumber, washed

salt and freshly ground pepper

25 g (1 oz) butter or margarine

1 onion, skinned and chopped

30 ml (2 tbsp) chopped fresh mint

50 g (2 oz) fresh white breadcrumbs

1 egg yolk

1.4 kg (3 lb) loin of lamb, boned

mint sprigs, to garnish

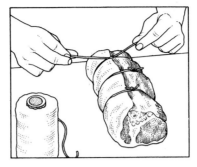

4 To serve, remove the string and carve into thick slices. Garnish with mint sprigs.

3 Roll up the meat and tie with fine string at regular intervals. Place the joint in a roasting tin and cook in the oven at 180°C (350°F) mark 4 for about 1 hour.

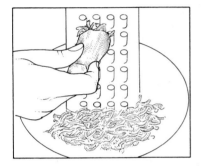

1 Coarsely grate the cucumber, sprinkle with salt and leave to stand for 30 minutes. Drain well. Melt the butter in a frying pan. Add onion and cook gently for about 5 minutes. Stir in the cucumber, mint, breadcrumbs, yolk and seasoning; cool for 30 minutes.

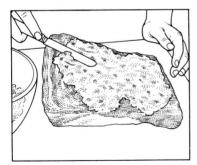

2 Lay the lamb out flat, fat side down, and spread the cold stuffing over the lamb.

21

VEAL IN MARSALA

$\boxed{0.25}$ £ £ $\boxed{301 \text{ cals}}$

Serves 6

6 small veal escalopes, about 75 g (3 oz) each

salt and freshly ground pepper

flour, for coating

60 ml (4 tbsp) vegetable oil

50 g (2 oz) butter

1 onion, skinned and finely chopped

175 g (6 oz) button mushrooms, wiped and sliced

90 ml (6 tbsp) Marsala

90 ml (6 tbsp) chicken stock

5 ml (1 tsp) arrowroot

lemon wedges, to garnish

1 Trim each escalope to remove any skin. Place well apart between sheets of non-stick paper, or heavy duty cling film.

2 Bat out well, using a meat mallet, rolling pin or heavy-based pan, until the escalopes are very thin. Remove paper or film.

3 Toss the veal in the seasoned flour. Then heat the oil and butter in a large sauté or deep frying pan and brown the veal well on all sides.

4 Push to the side of the pan and brown the onion and mushrooms in the residual fat. Add the Marsala, stock and bring to the boil; season lightly.

5 Cover the pan and cook gently for 5–10 minutes or until the veal is quite tender. Transfer to a serving dish, cover and keep warm.

6 Mix the arrowroot to a smooth paste with a little water. Stir into the pan juices off the heat, then bring slowly to the boil, stirring all the time. Cook for 1 minute, adjust seasoning and spoon over the veal. Garnish with lemon wedges.

Marsala
This famous Sicilian wine is made from a blend of local wines, brandy and unfermented grape juice. There are dry as well as sweet Marsalas, though the sweet variety used for classic Italian dishes, such as *zabaglione*, is most widely available.

Though it is a dessert wine, it is also an effective pick-me-up at any time of day.

WIENER SCHNITZEL
(VIENNESE VEAL ESCALOPES)

| 0.20 | £ | 398 cals |

Serves 4

4 veal escalopes, about 100 g (4 oz) each

salt and freshly ground pepper

1 egg, size 2, beaten

150 g (5 oz) fresh breadcrumbs

75 g (3 oz) butter or margarine

30 ml (2 tbsp) vegetable oil

lemon wedges and chopped fresh parsley, to garnish

1 Place each escalope between 2 sheets of dampened greaseproof paper and bat out thinly with a rolling pin.

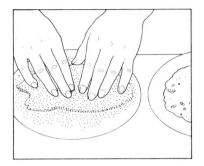

2 Sprinkle the meat with salt and pepper to taste. Coat in the beaten egg, then in the breadcrumbs, pressing the crumbs on well.

3 Melt the butter with the oil in a large frying pan. Add the escalopes, 2 at a time, and fry for about 2 minutes on each side, until golden. Drain on absorbent kitchen paper and keep warm while cooking the remainder.

4 Serve the schnitzels hot, garnished with lemon wedges dipped in chopped parsley.

23

CHICKEN WITH TARRAGON SAUCE

0.30	346 cals

Serves 6

6 chicken breasts, skinned

75 g (3 oz) butter or margarine

25 g (1 oz) plain flour

450 ml ($\frac{3}{4}$ pint) chicken stock

30 ml (2 tbsp) tarragon vinegar

10 ml (2 tsp) French mustard

5 ml (1 tsp) fresh chopped tarragon or 2.5 ml ($\frac{1}{2}$ tsp) dried

45 ml (3 tbsp) grated Parmesan cheese

salt and freshly ground pepper

150 ml (5 fl oz) single cream

tarragon sprigs, to garnish

1 In a covered pan, slowly fry the chicken breasts in 50 g (2 oz) butter for about 20 minutes until tender, turning once.

2 Meanwhile, melt the remaining butter in a pan, stir in the flour and gradually add the stock and vinegar. Stir in the mustard, tarragon and cheese; bring to the boil. Season with salt and pepper, simmer for 3 minutes.

3 Remove from the heat and add the cream. Heat gently without boiling. To serve, place the drained chicken on a serving dish, spoon over the sauce and garnish.

CORONATION CHICKEN

1.10	£	640 cals

Serves 8

2.3 kg (5 lb) cold cooked chicken
15 ml (1 tbsp) vegetable oil
1 small onion, skinned and chopped
15 ml (1 tbsp) mild curry paste
15 ml (1 tbsp) tomato purée
100 ml (4 fl oz) red wine
1 bay leaf
juice of $\frac{1}{2}$ lemon
4 canned apricot halves, finely chopped
300 ml ($\frac{1}{2}$ pint) mayonnaise
100 ml (4 fl oz) whipping cream
salt and freshly ground pepper
watercress sprigs, to garnish

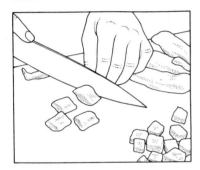

CORONATION CHICKEN
This delicious recipe – diced cold chicken tossed in a curried apricot mayonnaise – was created in 1953 by the Cordon Bleu School in London, in honour of the coronation of Queen Elizabeth II.

If you prefer, you can garnish the dish with sliced cucumber.

4 Toss the chicken pieces in the sauce and transfer to a serving dish. To serve, garnish with fresh watercress sprigs.

1 Remove the skin from the chicken. Then remove all the meat and dice, making sure to discard all the bones.

2 Make the curry sauce. Heat the oil in a small pan. Add the onion and cook for about 3 minutes, or until softened. Add the curry paste, tomato purée, wine, bay leaf and lemon juice. Simmer, uncovered, for about 10 minutes until well reduced. Strain and leave to cool for 30 minutes.

3 Press the chopped apricots through a sieve or use a blender or food processor to produce a purée. Beat the cooled curry sauce into the mayonnaise with the apricot purée. Lightly whip the cream and fold into the mixture. Season; add extra lemon juice, if necessary.

TURKEY PAPRIKA WITH PASTA

0.40	385 cals

Serves 4

30 ml (2 tbsp) vegetable oil

75 g (3 oz) onion, skinned and sliced

450 g (1 lb) turkey breasts

10 ml (2 tsp) paprika

450 ml ($\frac{3}{4}$ pint) chicken stock

salt and freshly ground pepper

1 green pepper, cored, seeded and sliced

100 g (4 oz) small pasta shapes

142 ml (5 fl oz) soured cream

paprika, to garnish

1 Heat the oil in a large sauté pan and fry the onion for 5 minutes until golden brown.

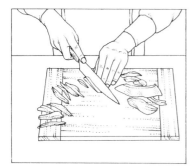

2 Skin the turkey breasts, discard any bone and cut flesh into small finger-sized pieces.

3 Add the turkey and paprika to the pan and toss over a moderate heat for 2 minutes.

4 Stir in the stock and seasoning and bring to the boil. Add the green pepper and pasta, cover and simmer gently for 15–20 minutes until turkey and pasta are tender.

5 Stir in the soured cream and adjust the seasoning. To serve, garnish with a little paprika.

PISSALADIÈRE

| 1.30 | £ | ✳ | 323 cals |

Serves 6

25 g (1 oz) butter or margarine

25 g (1 oz) lard

100 g (4 oz) plain flour

salt

30 ml (2 tbsp) water

450 g (1 lb) onions, skinned and finely sliced

2 garlic cloves, skinned and crushed

90 ml (6 tbsp) vegetable oil

225 g (8 oz) tomatoes, skinned

30 ml (2 tbsp) tomato purée

5 ml (1 tsp) fresh herbs (e.g. marjoram, thyme or sage)

freshly ground pepper

anchovy fillets and black olives

1 Make the pastry. Cut the butter or margarine and the lard into pieces and add these to the plain flour and a pinch of salt.

2 Mix until the mixture resembles fine breadcrumbs. Add water and mix until it forms a smooth dough. Wrap and chill in a refrigerator for 15 minutes.

3 When the dough is cool, roll out the pastry and use to line a 20.5-cm (8-inch) plain flan ring. Bake blind in the oven at 200°C (400°F) mark 6 for 20 minutes.

4 Meanwhile, make the filling. Fry onions and garlic in the oil in a large saucepan for 10 minutes until very soft but not brown.

5 Slice the tomatoes, add to the pan and continue cooking for 10 minutes until the liquid has evaporated. Stir in the tomato purée, herbs and seasoning.

6 Turn the mixture into the flan case. Brush with a little oil and cook in the oven at 200°C (400°F) mark 6 for 20 minutes.

7 To serve, garnish the pissaladière with a lattice of anchovy fillets and the black olives. Serve either hot or cold.

DRESSED CRAB

0.30 $\quad$ £ £

151–227 cals

Serves 2–3

shell and meat from 1 medium
(900-g/2-lb) cooked crab

salt and freshly ground pepper

15 ml (1 tbsp) lemon juice

30 ml (2 tbsp) fresh white breadcrumbs

1 egg, hard-boiled

chopped fresh parsley

lettuce or endive, to serve

1 Using two forks, flake all the
white meat from the crab, re-
moving any shell or membrane.
Season, adding about 5 ml (1 tsp)
lemon juice.

2 Pound brown meat and work
in the breadcrumbs with the
remaining lemon juice and seasoning. Adjust seasonings to taste.

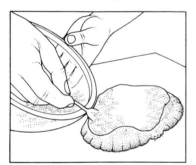

3 Using a small spoon, put the
white meat in both ends of the
crab's empty shell, making sure
that it is well piled up into the
shell. Keep the inside edges neat.

4 Then spoon the brown meat in
a neat line down the centre,
between the two sections of white
crabmeat.

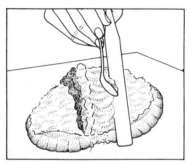

5 Hold a blunt knife between the
white and brown crabmeat and
carefully spoon lines of parsley,
sieved egg yolk and chopped egg
white across crab, moving knife as
you go to keep a neat edge. Serve
the stuffed shell on a bed of
lettuce or endive, surrounded by
the small legs.

28

MONKFISH AND MUSSEL BROCHETTES

0.40	£ £	365 cals

Serves 6

900 g (2 lb) monkfish, skinned and boned

36 mussels, cooked

18 rashers streaky bacon, rinded and halved

50 g (2 oz) butter, melted

60 ml (4 tbsp) chopped parsley

finely grated rind and juice of 1 lime or lemon

4 garlic cloves, skinned and crushed

salt and freshly ground pepper

shredded lettuce, bay leaves, and lime or lemon wedges, to garnish

1 Cut the fish into 42 cubes. Using a sharp knife, shell the mussels. Reserve the mussels and discard the shells.

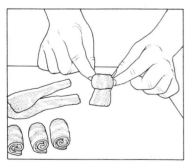

2 Roll the bacon rashers up neatly. Thread the cubed fish, mussels and bacon alternately on to six oiled kebab skewers.

3 Mix together the melted butter, parsley, lime rind and juice, garlic and salt and pepper to taste. (Take care when adding salt as both the mussels and the bacon are naturally salty.)

4 Place the brochettes on an oiled grill or barbecue rack. Brush with the butter mixture, then grill under a moderate grill for 15 minutes. Turn the brochettes frequently during cooking and brush with the butter mixture with each turn.

5 Arrange the hot brochettes on a serving platter lined with shredded lettuce. Garnish with bay leaves and lime wedges and serve at once with saffron rice, if liked.

PREPARING AND COOKING FRESH MUSSELS

When buying fresh mussels from the fishmonger, buy a good dozen more than you need to allow for those that are open. As soon as you get the mussels home, put them in a deep bowl of cold water and leave to soak for about 1 hour, changing the water several times. If any of the mussels are still open after this time, throw them away. Scrub the closed mussels clean with a stiff brush, scraping off any encrustations with a knife. Put them in a large pan with about 150 ml ($\frac{1}{4}$ pint) dry white wine or wine and water, garlic, herbs and seasoning to taste. Bring to the boil, then cover and simmer for 5–7 minutes until the shells open; discard any that do not.

TALI MACHCHLI
(SPICED GRILLED MACKEREL)

0.40*	🍳 f	470 cals

* plus 2 hours marinating

Serves 4

4 fresh mackerel, each weighing about 275 g (10 oz), gutted and cleaned

juice of 1 lemon

60 ml (4 tbsp) chopped fresh coriander

10 ml (2 tsp) garam masala

5 ml (1 tsp) ground cumin

5 ml (1 tsp) chilli powder

salt and freshly ground pepper

50 ml (2 fl oz) ghee or melted butter

lemon wedges, to serve

1 First bone the mackerel. With a sharp knife, cut off the heads just behind the gills. Extend the cut along the belly to both ends of the fish so that the fish can be opened out.

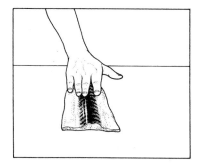

2 Place the fish flat on a board, skin side facing upwards. With the heel of your hand, press along the backbone to loosen it.

3 Turn the fish right way up and lift out the backbone, using the tip of the knife if necessary to help pull the bone away from the flesh cleanly. Discard the bone.

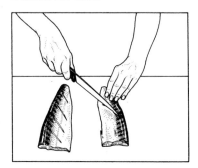

4 Remove the tail and cut each fish in half lengthways, then wash under cold running water and pat dry with absorbent kitchen paper. Score the skin side in several places with a knife.

5 In a jug, mix together the lemon juice, half of the coriander, the garam masala, cumin, chilli powder and salt and pepper to taste.

6 Put the mackerel in a grill pan and pour over the marinade. Cover and leave at cool room temperature for 2 hours, turning the fish once and brushing with the marinade.

7 When ready to cook, brush half of the ghee over the skin side of the mackerel. Cook under a preheated moderate grill for 5 minutes, then turn the fish over and brush with the remaining ghee. Grill for a further 5 minutes.

8 Transfer the fish to a warmed platter and sprinkle with the remaining coriander. Serve immediately, accompanied by lemon wedges.

TALI MACHCHLI
The spicy lemon marinade used in this recipe goes especially well with oily fish such as mackerel. In India there are numerous different varieties of both fresh- and sea-water fish, none of which are available here. The marinade can be used instead for familiar fish: fillets of plaice, haddock or cod, or even cubes of thick white monkfish, turbot or hake make excellent kebabs, especially when cooked outside on the barbecue.

WALDORF SALAD

$\boxed{0.40}$ £ $\boxed{402 \text{ cals}}$

Serves 4

450 g (1 lb) eating apples

juice of 1 lemon

5 ml (1 tsp) sugar

150 ml ($\frac{1}{4}$ pint) mayonnaise

$\frac{1}{2}$ head celery, washed, trimmed and sliced

50 g (2 oz) walnuts, chopped

1 lettuce

few walnut halves, to garnish (optional)

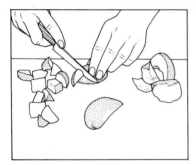

1 Core the apples, slice one and dice the rest. Dip the slices in lemon juice to prevent discoloration of the fruit.

2 Toss the diced apples in 30 ml (2 tbsp) lemon juice, the sugar and 15 ml (1 tbsp) mayonnaise and leave to stand for about 30 minutes.

3 Just before serving, add the sliced celery, chopped walnuts and the remaining mayonnaise, and toss together.

4 Serve in a bowl lined with lettuce leaves and garnish with the apple slices and a few walnut halves, if liked.

PASTA, PRAWN AND APPLE SALAD

0.30* £ 176 cals

* plus 2–3 hours chilling

Serves 6

175 g (6 oz) pasta shells

150 ml ($\frac{1}{4}$ pint) unsweetened apple juice

5 ml (1 tsp) chopped fresh mint

5 ml (1 tsp) white wine vinegar

salt and freshly ground pepper

225 g (8 oz) peeled prawns

225 g (8 oz) crisp eating apples

lettuce leaves

paprika, to garnish

1 Cook the pasta in boiling salted water for 10–15 minutes until tender. Drain well, rinse in cold running water and drain again.

2 Meanwhile, make the dressing. Whisk together the apple juice, mint, vinegar and seasoning.

3 Dry the prawns with absorbent kitchen paper. Quarter, core and roughly chop the apples. Stir the prawns, apple and cooked pasta into the dressing until well mixed. Cover tightly with cling film and refrigerate for 2–3 hours.

4 Wash the lettuce leaves, dry and shred finely. Place a little lettuce in six individual serving dishes. Spoon the prawn salad on top and dust with paprika.

CUCUMBER SALAD

1.10*	128 cals

* plus 4 hours or overnight chilling

Serves 4

1 large cucumber
salt and freshly ground pepper
45 ml (3 tbsp) white wine vinegar
45 ml (3 tbsp) water
25 g (1 oz) sugar
2.5 ml ($\frac{1}{2}$ tsp) dried dillweed
150 ml ($\frac{1}{4}$ pint) soured cream
150 ml ($\frac{1}{4}$ pint) thick set natural yogurt
30 ml (2 tbsp) snipped chives

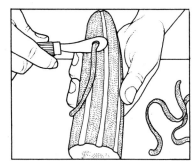 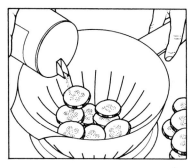

1 Using a cannelle knife or vegetable peeler, peel lengthways strips off the cucumber. Slice the cucumber thinly into rings.

2 Put the cucumber slices in a colander, sprinkling each layer liberally with salt. Cover with a plate, place heavy weights on top, then leave for 30 minutes.

3 Meanwhile make the dressing. Put the vinegar, water and sugar in a saucepan and heat gently. Boil for 1 minute, remove from the heat and leave to cool.

4 Rinse the cucumber slices quickly under cold running water, then pat dry; place in a bowl. Stir the dill into the dressing with plenty of pepper, then pour over the cucumber. Cover and chill for 4 hours or overnight, turning the slices occasionally.

5 Mix the soured cream and yogurt with the chives; season to taste. Arrange the cucumber on a serving plate; spoon the dressing in the centre. Serve chilled.

RADICCHIO AND ALFALFA SALAD

0.15	141–212 cals

Serves 4–6

2 heads of radicchio

50–75 g (2–3 oz) alfalfa sprouts

90 ml (6 tbsp) olive or vegetable oil

30 ml (2 tbsp) white wine vinegar

15 ml (1 tbsp) single cream (optional)

1 small garlic clove, skinned and crushed

1.25 ml ($\frac{1}{4}$ tsp) granulated sugar

salt and freshly ground pepper

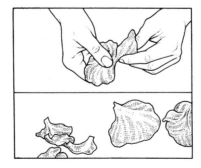

1 Tear the radicchio into bite-sized pieces. Wash, drain and pat dry on absorbent kitchen paper. Wash and dry the alfalfa sprouts.

2 Mix the alfalfa and radicchio together in a serving bowl. In a jug, whisk together the remaining ingredients, with salt and pepper to taste. Just before serving, pour over the radicchio and alfalfa and toss together.

CHILLI POTATO SALAD

0.35^* £ 448 cals

* plus 2 hours chilling

Serves 6

900 g (2 lb) even-sized new potatoes

1 medium green pepper

1 medium red pepper

200 ml (7 fl oz) vegetable oil

75 ml (5 tbsp) garlic vinegar

15 ml (1 tbsp) chilli seasoning

salt and freshly ground pepper

1 medium onion, skinned and chopped

30 ml (2 tbsp) sesame seeds

fresh coriander, to garnish

1 Scrub the potatoes and boil in their skins until tender; about 20 minutes. Drain well.

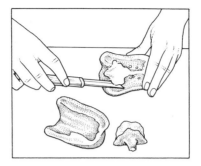

2 Meanwhile, halve, seed and chop the peppers. Blanch them in boiling water for 1–2 minutes. Drain well.

3 In a large bowl, whisk together the oil, vinegar, chilli seasoning and salt and pepper to taste.

4 Halve the potatoes if they are large, but do not peel them. While still hot, stir into the dressing with the onion and peppers. Cool, cover and chill in the refrigerator for about 2 hours.

5 Toast the sesame seeds under the grill, leave to cool, then stir through the salad. Taste and adjust the seasoning before serving, garnished with fresh coriander.

38

CHEF'S SALAD

0.15	£	690 cals

Serves 4

225 g (8 oz) ham

225 g (8 oz) cold cooked chicken

225 g (8 oz) Emmenthal cheese

1 Iceberg or Webb lettuce

2 eggs, hard-boiled, shelled and quartered

6 small tomatoes, halved, or 2 large tomatoes, quartered

3 spring onions, washed, trimmed and finely chopped

150 ml ($\frac{1}{4}$ pint) vinaigrette

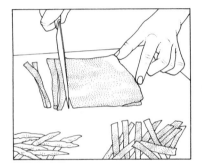

1 Using a sharp knife, cut the ham and the cold cooked chicken into fine strips and set aside.

2 Remove any rind from the cheese. Using a small sharp knife, carefully cut the cheese into small dice. Wash the lettuce under cold running water and pat it dry with absorbent kitchen paper.

3 Finely shred the leaves, or leave them whole, and use to line an oval serving dish.

4 To serve. Arrange the meat and cheese alternately around the edge of the dish. Add egg and tomatoes, sprinkle over the finely chopped spring onions and serve the dressing separately.

PARTY PASSION PAVLOVA

| 1.30 | 🍶 | 299–374 cals |

Serves 8–10

4 egg whites

pinch of salt

275 g (10 oz) caster sugar

5 ml (1 tsp) vanilla flavouring

6.25 ml ($1\frac{1}{4}$ tsp) cornflour

6.25 ml ($1\frac{1}{4}$ tsp) vinegar

4 kiwi fruit

4 satsumas or mandarin oranges

few thin slices of preserved or stem ginger

60 ml (4 tbsp) whisky

30 ml (2 tbsp) ginger wine or syrup from the stem ginger

300 ml ($\frac{1}{2}$ pint) double or whipping cream

150 ml ($\frac{1}{4}$ pint) thick, set yogurt or Quark

4 fresh passion fruit

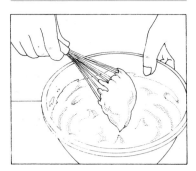

1 Put the egg whites in a large bowl and whisk until stiff and standing in peaks. Whisk in the salt and 125 g (4 oz) of the sugar until the meringue is glossy.

2 With a metal spoon, fold in another 125 g (4 oz) of the sugar with the vanilla flavouring, cornflour and vinegar.

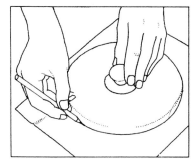

3 Draw a 25.5 cm (10 inch) circle on a large sheet of non-stick baking parchment. Place the paper, marked side down, on a baking sheet.

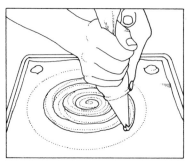

4 Spoon the meringue into a large piping bag fitted with a large plain nozzle. Pipe the meringue in a spiral, starting at the centre of the marked circle and working outwards towards the edge.

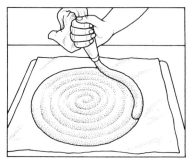

5 Pipe a second layer of meringue on top of the outer edge of the circle, to make a raised lip to prevent the topping spilling over the edge when serving.

6 Bake in the oven at 150°C (300°F) mark 2 for 1 hour until crisp and dry. With 2 fish slices or wide metal spatulas, lift the pavlova off the baking parchment and onto a wire rack. Leave to cool.

7 Meanwhile, prepare the topping. Peel the kiwi fruit and slice thinly. Peel the satsumas and divide into segments. Put the preserved or stem ginger in a bowl with the remaining sugar, the whisky and ginger wine or syrup. Add the prepared fruit and stir gently to mix. Whip the cream and yogurt together until thick.

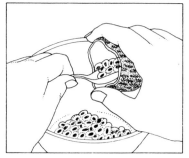

8 Just before serving, transfer the cold pavlova to a large serving platter. Spread the cream mixture in the centre, then arrange the fruit decoratively on top. Pour over any juices. Slice the passion fruit in half, scoop out the flesh with a teaspoon, then sprinkle over the top of the pavlova. Serve within 1 hour or the topping will make the pavlova too soft.

MERINGUE BASKET

6.00* 🥂 🥂 £ | 317–423 cals

* plus 20 minutes cooling

Serves 6–8

4 egg whites

225 g (8 oz) icing sugar

1 small pineapple

3 bananas

300 ml (10 fl oz) whipping cream

30 ml (2 tbsp) kirsch

coarsely grated chocolate,
   to decorate

1 Line three baking sheets with non-stick baking parchment (turn rimmed baking sheets upside down and use the bases), and draw a 19-cm ($7\frac{1}{2}$-inch) circle on each. Turn the paper over so that the pencilled circle is visible but does not come into contact with the meringues and mark them.

2 Place 3 egg whites in a clean, dry heatproof bowl, and place the bowl over a pan of simmering water. Sift in 175 g (6 oz) of the icing sugar.

3 Whisk the egg whites and sugar vigorously over the simmering water until the mixture stands in very stiff peaks. Do not allow the bowl to get too hot or the meringue will crust around edges.

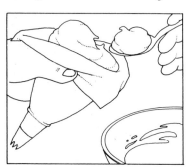

4 Fit a piping bag with a large star nozzle. Spoon in one third of the meringue mixture. Secure the paper to the baking sheets with a little meringue.

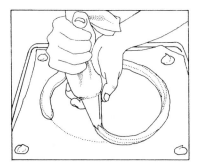

5 Pipe rings of meringue about 1 cm ($\frac{1}{2}$ inch) thick inside two of the circles on the paper.

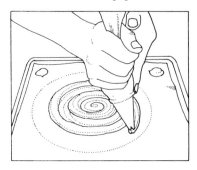

6 Fill the bag with the remaining meringue and, starting from centre, pipe a continuous coil of meringue on the third sheet of paper. Place all in the oven at 100°C (200°F) gas mark Low for $2\frac{1}{2}$–3 hours to dry out.

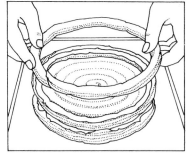

7 Use the remaining egg white and sugar to make meringue as before and put into the piping bag. Remove the cooked meringue rings from the paper and layer up on the base, piping a ring of fresh meringue between each. Return to oven for a further $1\frac{1}{2}$–2 hours. Slide on to a wire rack and peel off base paper when cool.

8 Cut the pineapple across into 1-cm ($\frac{1}{2}$-inch) slices and snip off skin. Cut out core and divide flesh into bite-size chunks. Peel bananas and cut into 1-cm ($\frac{1}{2}$-inch) slices. Mix the fruits together, reserving a little pineapple and banana for decoration.

9 Just before serving, stand the meringue shell on a flat serving plate. Lightly whip the cream and fold in the kirsch; spoon half into the base of the basket and top with the fruit. Whirl the remaining cream over the top and decorate with the reserved pineapple, banana and the grated chocolate.

MAKING MERINGUES

There are three basic types of meringue. *Meringue suisse* is the most common and the most simple—egg whites are stiffly whisked, then caster sugar is folded in. *Meringue cuite* is the type of meringue used for this basket. It is firmer than *meringue suisse* and therefore better able to hold up when filled with fruit and cream as here. Although its name suggests that it is cooked, it is in fact only whisked over hot water before being baked in the same way as *meringue suisse*. *Meringue italienne* is made by combining sugar syrup with egg whites; it is difficult to make, and mostly used by professionals.

FRESH APRICOT FLAN

1.30* 🝆 £ £ ✳ 384 cals

* plus 2 hours chilling

Serves 6

150 g (5 oz) plain flour

50 g (2 oz) ground almonds

75 g (3 oz) butter or block margarine, cut into pieces

1 egg yolk mixed with 15 ml (1 tbsp) water

2 eggs

150 ml (5 fl oz) single cream

15 ml (1 tbsp) caster sugar

few drops almond flavouring

120 ml (8 tbsp) apricot jam, sieved

450 g (1 lb) fresh apricots, skinned, halved and stoned or one 411-g (14-oz) can apricot halves, drained

15 ml (1 tbsp) lemon juice

15 ml (1 tbsp) almond-flavoured liqueur

1 Mix the flour in a bowl with half the ground almonds. Rub in the butter until the mixture resembles fine breadcrumbs. Bind to a firm dough with the egg yolk mixture; knead lightly until smooth.

2 Roll out the dough on a lightly floured working surface and use to line a 22-cm (8½-inch) loose-bottomed French fluted flan tin. Bake 'blind' in the oven at 190°C (375°F) mark 5 for 15–20 minutes until set but not browned.

3 Meanwhile, mix the eggs, cream, sugar, remaining ground almonds and almond flavouring.

4 Warm the jam gently in a small saucepan. When the flan is set, spread 45 ml (3 tbsp) jam over base. Pour cream mixture into flan.

5 Reduce the oven to 170°C (325°F) mark 3; return flan to it for 20 minutes or until the filling is just set; leave for about 1 hour to cool.

6 Arrange the apricot halves neatly over the custard filling in the flan.

7 Add the lemon juice to the remaining jam together with the liqueur and reduce the mixture to a glaze. Brush over the apricots to cover them completely. Refrigerate for 2 hours before serving.

STRAWBERRY CUSTARD FLAN

$\boxed{0.35^*}$ ⊟ £ £ $\boxed{\text{445–556 cals}}$

*plus 1 hour 10 minutes cooling and about $1\frac{1}{2}$ hours chilling

Serves 6–8

175 g (6 oz) plain flour

125 g (4 oz) caster sugar

125 g (4 oz) butter or block margarine

3 eggs

40 g ($1\frac{1}{2}$ oz) cornflour

450 ml ($\frac{3}{4}$ pint) milk

few drops of vanilla flavouring

350 g (12 oz) strawberries, hulled

pouring cream, to serve

1 Mix the flour with 25 g (1 oz) sugar in a bowl, then rub in the fat until the mixture resembles fine breadcrumbs. Bind to a soft dough with 1 egg. Knead lightly on a floured work surface until just smooth.

2 Roll out the pastry on a floured work surface and use to line a 23-cm (9-inch) flan dish. Refrigerate for 30 minutes. Prick the base of the flan and bake blind in the oven at 200°C (400°F) mark 6 for 20 minutes or until pale golden and cooked through. Cool in the dish for 30–40 minutes.

3 Mix the cornflour to a smooth paste with a little of the milk. Separate the remaining eggs and mix the egg yolks with the cornflour paste. Put the rest of the milk in a saucepan with the remaining sugar and the vanilla flavouring. Bring to the boil, then remove from the heat and pour in the cornflour mixture. Return to the boil, stirring, and boil for 2 minutes until thickened. Cover with damp greaseproof paper and cool for 30 minutes. (Whisk if necessary to remove lumps.)

4 Thinly slice the strawberries into the base of the flan, reserving a few for decoration. Whisk the egg whites until stiff and fold into the cold custard mixture. Smooth the custard mixture evenly over the strawberries. Refrigerate for 1 hour until set.

5 Serve the flan decorated with the reserved strawberry slices, preferably within 2 hours of completion. Serve with cream.

STRAWBERRY SHORTCAKES

1.30	£ £ ✳*	611 cals

* after stage 6

Serves 6

275 g (10 oz) self-raising flour

7.5 ml (1½ tsp) baking powder

good pinch of salt

75 g (3 oz) butter, cut into nut-size pieces

50 g (2 oz) caster sugar

1 egg, beaten

few drops vanilla flavouring

75–90 ml (5–6 tbsp) milk

450 g (1 lb) fresh strawberries, 6 set aside, the remainder hulled

30 ml (2 tbsp) orange-flavoured liqueur

30 ml (2 tbsp) icing sugar

300 ml (10 fl oz) double or whipping cream

45 ml (3 tbsp) redcurrant jelly

1 Brush a little melted lard over a large flat baking sheet; leave to cool for about 5 minutes. Dust the surface lightly with flour.

2 Sift the flour, baking powder and salt into a bowl. Rub in the butter until the mixture resembles breadcrumbs. Stir in the caster sugar.

3 Make a well in the centre of the dry ingredients and add the egg, vanilla flavouring and milk. Using a palette knife, cut through the dry ingredients until evenly blended, then quickly and lightly bring the mixture together using the fingertips of one hand.

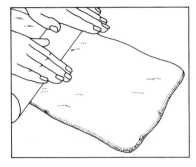

4 Turn the dough out on to a lightly floured surface and knead gently until just smooth. Roll out to a thickness of 1 cm (½ inch) and cut out six 9-cm (3½-inch) fluted rounds.

5 Gather up the scraps, knead lightly and roll out again. Place on the prepared baking sheet.

6 Brush the tops of the rounds with milk—don't let it trickle down the sides. Bake in the oven at 230°C (450°F) mark 8 for about 11 minutes or until the shortcakes are well risen and golden brown. Remove from the oven and keep warm.

7 Thickly slice half the strawberries. Put into a bowl and add the liqueur. Sieve in half the icing sugar.

8 With a fork, lightly crush the remaining strawberries and sieve in the rest of the icing sugar. Whip the cream until it just holds its shape and stir in the crushed strawberries.

9 Cut the shortcakes in half while they are still warm. Carefully run the point of a sharp knife from the side of the shortcake into the centre.

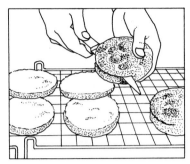

10 Rotate the shortcake and saw with the sharp knife until the cake is cut in two.

11 Spoon half the cream on to the shortcake bases and cover with the sliced strawberries. Spoon over the remaining cream and replace the shortcake tops.

12 Put the redcurrant jelly into a small pan and heat gently until liquid. Cool for 5–10 minutes, then brush over the shortcakes. Decorate with whole strawberries.

——————— VARIATION ———————

Any other soft fruits such as raspberries, loganberries, blackberries, bilberries or redcurrants can be used as an alternative filling for these delicious shortcakes. Skinned and roughly chopped peaches and nectarines would also be delicious. The tart flavour of berries or currants can be counteracted by adding a little more sugar.

SQUIDGY CHOCOLATE MOUSSE CAKE

1.30* 🗇 £ £ ✳* 586 cals

* plus 1 hour cooling and overnight chilling; freeze after stage 6

Serves 8

450 g (1 lb) plain chocolate

45 ml (3 tbsp) orange-flavoured liqueur

9 eggs, 5 of them separated

150 g (5 oz) caster sugar

100 g (4 oz) unsalted butter, softened

blanched julienne strips of orange rind and grated chocolate, to decorate

1 Grease a 20-cm (8-inch) spring-release tin, line with greaseproof paper and grease the paper.

2 Break half the chocolate into a heatproof bowl and place over a pan of simmering water and stir gently until the chocolate has melted. Stir in 15 ml (1 tbsp) liqueur, then remove from the heat.

3 Using an electric whisk, whisk five egg yolks and the sugar together until thick and creamy, then beat in the butter a little at a time until smooth. Beat in the melted chocolate until smooth.

4 Whisk the five egg whites until stiff, then fold into the chocolate mixture. Turn into the prepared tin and bake in the oven at 180°C (350°F) mark 4 for 40 minutes until risen and firm. Leave the cake to cool in the tin for 1 hour.

5 Make the top layer: melt the remaining chocolate as before, then stir in the remaining liqueur. Remove from the heat, cool for 1–2 minutes. Separate the remaining eggs and beat the egg yolks into the chocolate mixture. Whisk the egg whites until stiff, then fold into the chocolate mixture.

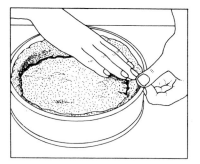

6 Press the crust down on the baked cake with your fingers and pour the top layer over it. Refrigerate overnight.

7 The next day, remove the cake carefully from the tin and put on to a serving plate.

8 Arrange blanched strips of orange rind around the outside edge and decorate with grated chocolate.

48

CREAM CROWDIE

0.30^* £ 481 cals

* plus 1 hour refrigeration and 30 minutes standing time

Serves 4

50 g (2 oz) medium oatmeal

300 ml (10 fl oz) double cream

60 ml (4 tbsp) clear honey

45 ml (3 tbsp) whisky

350 g (12 oz) fresh raspberries, hulled

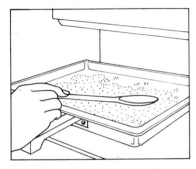

1 Place the oatmeal in a grill pan (without the rack) and toast until golden brown, turning occasionally with a spoon. Leave for 15 minutes until cool.

2 Whip the cream until just standing in soft peaks, then stir in the honey, whisky and cooled toasted oatmeal.

3 Reserve a few raspberries for decoration, then layer up the remaining raspberries and fresh cream mixture in four tall glasses. Cover with cling film and refrigerate for at least 1 hour.

4 Allow to come to room temperature for 30 minutes before serving. Decorate each glass with the reserved raspberries.

CROWDIE

In Scotland, *crowdie* can mean a cream cheese or a kind of porridge. This recipe for cream crowdie is so called because it contains oatmeal, which the Scots use for making porridge.

SHERRIED APRICOT TRIFLE

$\boxed{1.00^*}$ $\boxed{573 \text{ cals}}$

* plus cooling, setting and overnight chilling

Serves 8–10

410 g (14½ oz) can apricot halves in natural juice

127 g (4½ oz) packet orange- or tangerine-flavoured jelly

350 g (12 oz) Madeira cake

300 ml (½ pint) sherry

1 egg

2 egg yolks

25 g (1 oz) caster sugar

15 ml (1 tbsp) cornflour

450 ml (¾ pint) milk

300 ml (½ pint) double or whipping cream

few strips of angelica and some glacé cherries, to decorate

1 Drain the apricots and measure the juice. Make up the jelly according to packet instructions, using the apricot juice as part of the measured liquid. Leave in a cool place until cold and just beginning to set.

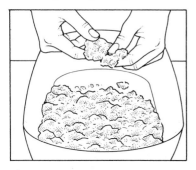

2 Meanwhile break up the cake with your fingers and place in the bottom of a glass serving dish. Pour over the sherry, place the apricots on top, reserving one for decoration, cover and leave to stand while making the custard.

3 Make the custard. Put the egg and egg yolks in a bowl with the sugar and whisk lightly together. Add the cornflour and a few tablespoons of the milk and whisk again until combined.

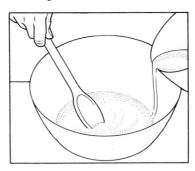

4 Scald the milk in a heavy-based saucepan. Pour on to the egg mixture, stirring constantly, then return the custard to the rinsed-out pan. Cook over low to moderate heat, stirring all the time until the custard thickens and coats the back of the spoon. Pour immediately into a bowl, cover the surface of the custard closely with cling film and leave until cold.

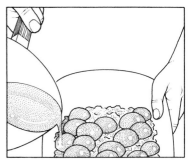

5 Pour the cold, setting jelly over the apricots in the serving dish, spreading it evenly, then chill in the refrigerator until set.

6 Pour the cold custard over the jelly, cover closely with cling film and chill overnight.

7 Whip the cream until stiff, then swirl or pipe over the trifle leaving the centre uncovered. Decorate with the remaining apricot, angelica 'stalks', and glacé cherry 'flowers'. Serve chilled.

SHERRIED APRICOT TRIFLE

Trifle is an old-fashioned English dish, traditionally served at Sunday tea time. Every English family has its own version, but the authentic English trifle which was so popular in Victorian days was a simple layered concoction of Madeira cake soaked in sherry, almond-flavoured macaroons or ratafias, a rich egg custard and a topping of thickly whipped cream. Today's modern trifle with fruit and jelly would have been frowned upon by the Victorians.

The essence of making a good trifle lies in using a large quantity of sherry for soaking the Madeira cake base. It may seem extravagant when you are making it, but unless you use the amount specified in the recipe, you will not get the proper 'boozy' flavour, which is vital to a really good special-occasion trifle like this.

COFFEE BAVARIAN CREAM

1.45^* 🄴 £ £ 555 cals

* plus 3 hours or overnight chilling
Serves 6

125 g (4 oz) roasted coffee beans
900 ml ($1\frac{1}{2}$ pints) milk
6 egg yolks
75 g (3 oz) caster sugar
20 ml (4 tsp) powdered gelatine
60 ml (4 tbsp) water
300 ml ($\frac{1}{2}$ pint) double cream
30 ml (2 tbsp) coffee-flavoured
  liqueur
coffee dragees and coarsely
  grated chocolate, to decorate

1 Put the coffee beans in a
saucepan and place over low
heat for 2–3 minutes, shaking the
pan frequently. Off the heat, pour
all the milk into the pan, then
return to the heat and bring to the
boil. Remove from the heat, cover
the pan and leave to infuse for at
least 30 minutes.

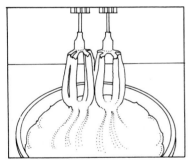

2 Beat the egg yolks and caster
sugar in a bowl until thick and
light in colour. The beaters should
leave a ribbon trail on the surface
of the mixture when lifted.

3 Strain on the milk and stir
well. Pour into the rinsed out
pan and stir over low heat for 10
minutes. Do *not* boil. Strain into a
large bowl; cool for 20 minutes.

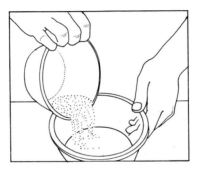

4 Sprinkle the gelatine over the
water in a small heatproof
bowl. Leave for 5 minutes until
spongy, then stand the bowl in a
pan of gently simmering water and
heat until dissolved.

5 Stir the gelatine into the
custard. Stand this in a roasting tin of cold water and ice
cubes. Stir until the mixture is
cool and about to set.

6 Lightly whip half of the cream
to the thick pouring stage,
then fold into the custard. Pour
into a lightly oiled 1.4 litre (2 pint)
moule-à-manqué cake tin or
soufflé dish. Chill for at least 3
hours or overnight until
completely set.

7 With dampened fingers, gently
ease the edges of the cream
away from the tin. Turn the cream
out on to a flat plate, shaking the
tin or dish gently until the cream
moves and loosens inside the tin.
Carefully ease off the tin and slide
the cream into the centre of the
plate.

8 Whip the remaining cream
until stiff, then gradually
whisk in the coffee liqueur. Spoon
into a piping bag fitted with a 1 cm
($\frac{1}{2}$ inch) star nozzle and pipe
rosettes around the top edge of the
cream. Decorate with coffee
dragees and grated chocolate.
Serve chilled.

SUMMER FRUIT SALAD

1.20*	£ £	117–176 cals

* plus 30 minutes cooling

Serves 4–6

100 g (4 oz) sugar
200 ml (7 fl oz) water
few fresh mint sprigs
1 strip of orange peel
225 g (8 oz) fresh strawberries
225 g (8 oz) fresh raspberries
1 small Ogen melon
30 ml (2 tbsp) orange-flavoured liqueur
30 ml (2 tbsp) finely chopped fresh mint
few whole fresh mint leaves, to decorate

1 Put the sugar in a heavy-based pan, add the water and heat gently for 5–10 minutes until the sugar has dissolved, stirring occasionally.

2 Add the mint sprigs and orange peel, then boil the syrup rapidly for 5 minutes, without stirring. Remove from the heat and leave for about 1 hour until completely cold.

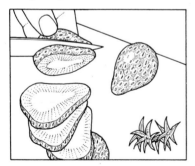

3 Meanwhile, prepare the fruit. Hull the strawberries, then slice them lengthways.

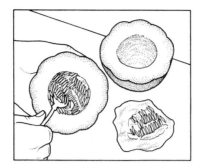

4 Leave the raspberries whole. Cut the melon in half, scoop out and discard the seeds.

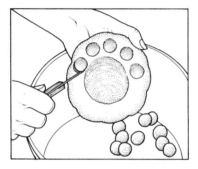

5 Cut the flesh into balls using a melon baller. Remove the mint sprigs and orange peel from the cold syrup, then stir in the liqueur and chopped mint.

6 Put the fruit in a serving bowl, pour over the syrup, then carefully fold together. Chill in the refrigerator for at least 30 minutes. Serve chilled, decorated with whole fresh mint leaves.

MELONS

The Ogen melon specified in this Summer Fruit Salad is available most of the year from specialist greengrocers and markets. The name 'Ogen' comes from the kibbutz in Israel where these melons were first grown.

Ogen melons are well worth looking for, because their flesh is very sweet—perfect for summer fruit salads, and also for winter desserts when other fresh fruits are scarce. Ogen melons are easily identified by their yellowy-green, stripy skins and their almost perfect round shape. Most Ogen melons are small enough for 1 serving, but large ones are also available which will serve 2–3 people. Both sizes are ideal for making into melon baskets—a pretty way to serve a fruit salad such as the one on this page. If you buy small Ogens, make individual baskets for each place setting; large Ogens, like honeydew melons, make spectacular table centrepieces.

To make a melon basket
1 Level the base of the melon so that it will stand upright.
2 With the tip of a sharp knife, score horizontally around the centre of the melon, keeping the line as straight as possible.
3 Cut down from the top of the melon to the scored line, working about 1 cm ($\frac{1}{2}$ inch) to one side of the centre.
4 Cut through the scored line on one side so that a wedge-shaped piece of melon is removed.
5 Repeat steps 3 and 4 so that both sides are removed.
6 Carefully scrape away the melon flesh inside the 'handle' left in the centre.
7 Scoop out and discard the seeds, then remove the flesh in the bottom half of the basket with a melon baller or sharp knife. Combine with the cut flesh from the reserved wedges.

STRAWBERRIES WITH RASPBERRY SAUCE

0.20* | 91 cals

* plus at least 30 minutes chilling

Serves 6

900 g (2 lb) small strawberries

450 g (1 lb) raspberries

50 g (2 oz) icing sugar

1 Hull the strawberries and place them in individual serving dishes.

2 Purée the raspberries in a blender or food processor until just smooth, then work through a nylon sieve into a bowl to remove the pips.

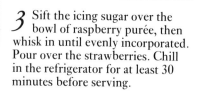

3 Sift the icing sugar over the bowl of raspberry purée, then whisk in until evenly incorporated. Pour over the strawberries. Chill in the refrigerator for at least 30 minutes before serving.

STRAWBERRIES WITH RASPBERRY SAUCE

Freshly picked raspberries freeze successfully (unlike strawberries which tend to lose texture and shape due to their high water content). If you have raspberries which are slightly overripe or misshapen, the best way to freeze them is as a purée; this takes up less space in the freezer and is immensely useful for making quick desserts and sauces at the last minute. For this recipe, for example, you can freeze the purée up to 12 months in advance, then it will only take a few minutes to put the dessert together after the purée has thawed. The purée can be frozen with or without the icing sugar.

ALMOND PEACH BRÛLÉES

| 0.20* | £ £ | 290 cals |

* plus at least 9 hours chilling

Serves 6

6 large, ripe peaches
30 ml (2 tbsp) lemon juice
150 ml (5 fl oz) double cream
30 ml (2 tbsp) icing sugar
30 ml (2 tbsp) almond-flavoured liqueur or few drops of almond flavouring
142 ml (5 fl oz) soured cream
90–120 ml (6–8 tbsp) demerara sugar

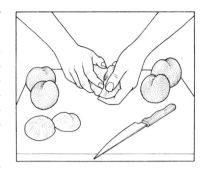

1 Peel the peaches by dipping them in boiling water for about 30 seconds. Plunge them immediately into cold water; peel off the skins. Cut the peaches in half. Twist to separate; remove stones. Thinly slice flesh, toss in lemon juice and set aside.

2 Whip the double cream with the icing sugar until it just holds its shape. Gradually whisk in the liqueur or almond flavouring. Fold in the soured cream and peach slices.

3 Divide this mixture between six 150-ml ($\frac{1}{4}$-pint) ramekin dishes. Cover and chill overnight. Sprinkle enough demerara sugar on top to form a covering.

4 Place under a hot grill for 3–4 minutes until the sugar has caramelised. Chill for about 1 hour.

BLACKBERRY ICE CREAM

$\boxed{0.40*}$ 🝆 £ ✳ $\boxed{436\text{ cals}}$

* plus 1 hour cooling, 9 hours freezing and 2 hours softening

Serves 6

450 g (1 lb) blackberries, fresh or frozen

30 ml (2 tbsp) thick honey

50 g (2 oz) caster sugar

410 g ($14\frac{1}{2}$ oz) can evaporated milk, chilled

150 ml ($\frac{1}{4}$ pint) double cream

30 ml (2 tbsp) orange-flavoured liqueur

45 ml (3 tbsp) lemon juice

single cream and wafer biscuits, to serve

1 Pick over fresh blackberries, wash and drain well. Place the berries in a small saucepan with the honey and sugar, cover the pan and cook gently for 5–10 minutes until soft.

2 Purée in a blender or food processor, then pass through a nylon sieve to remove pips. Leave to cool for about 1 hour.

3 Whip the evaporated milk until it thickens slightly, then whisk the cream to the same consistency and fold gently together. Stir in the fruit purée with the liqueur and lemon juice.

4 Pour into a container (not metal). Freeze for about 3 hours or until set to a mushy consistency.

5 Remove from the freezer and beat well to break down the ice crystals. Return to the freezer for at least 6 hours.

6 Allow the ice cream to 'come to' in the refrigerator for 2 hours. Scoop into individual glass dishes and serve with single cream and wafer biscuits.

GERANIUM GRAPE SORBET

| 1.00^* | 🥄 | ✳ | 160 cals |

* plus 3–4 hours freezing

Serves 6

100 g (4 oz) sugar

300 ml ($\frac{1}{2}$ pint) water

15 ml (1 tbsp) chopped rose- or lemon-scented geranium leaves

700 g ($1\frac{1}{2}$ lb) seedless green grapes

90 ml (6 tbsp) dry white vermouth

2 egg whites

green food colouring

rose- or lemon-scented geranium leaves, to decorate

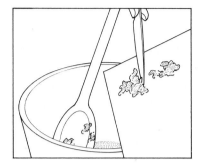

1 Make the sugar syrup. Dissolve the sugar in the water over a low heat. Bring to the boil and boil gently for 10 minutes. Add leaves, cover and cool.

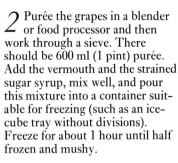

2 Purée the grapes in a blender or food processor and then work through a sieve. There should be 600 ml (1 pint) purée. Add the vermouth and the strained sugar syrup, mix well, and pour this mixture into a container suitable for freezing (such as an ice-cube tray without divisions). Freeze for about 1 hour until half frozen and mushy.

3 Turn the half frozen mixture into a large bowl and break up with a fork.

4 Whisk the egg whites until stiff and fold into the grape mixture. Tint a pale green using a few drops of food colouring. Return to the container and freeze for about 2–3 hours until firm. Serve straight from the freezer, decorated with geranium leaves.

Oranges en Surprise

$\boxed{0.50^*}$ £ £ ✳ $\boxed{392 \text{ cals}}$

* plus at least 4 hours (preferably overnight) freezing

Serves 6

6 large oranges

300 ml (10 fl oz) double cream

50 g (2 oz) icing sugar

90 ml (6 tbsp) orange-flavoured liqueur

90 ml (6 tbsp) chunky orange marmalade

fresh bay leaves or chocolate rose leaves, to decorate (optional)

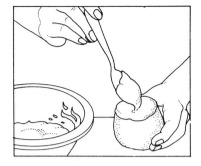

1 Cut a slice off the top of each orange and reserve. Scoop out all the flesh, pips and juice from the oranges and discard (the juice can be used for drinking or in other recipes). Wash, then dry thoroughly. Set aside.

2 Whip the cream with the icing sugar until standing in stiff peaks. Mix together the liqueur and marmalade, then fold into the cream until evenly distributed.

3 Spoon the cream mixture into the orange shells, mounding it up so that it protrudes over the top. Freeze for at least 4 hours, preferably overnight (to allow the flavours to develop). Serve straight from the freezer, decorated with reserved orange lids, bay or chocolate rose leaves.

ICED ORANGE SABAYON

$0.25*$ ☐ £ £ ✳ 282 cals

* plus 30 minutes cooling and 3–4 hours freezing

Serves 6

6 egg yolks

175 g (6 oz) demerara sugar

90 ml (6 tbsp) orange-flavoured liqueur

200 ml (7 fl oz) unsweetened orange juice

glacé cherries and candied peel, to decorate

1 Put the egg yolks and sugar in a bowl and beat together until pale and creamy. Stir in the liqueur and orange juice.

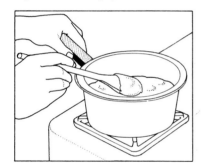

2 Pour into a medium-sized heavy-based saucepan. Stir over low heat until the mixture thickens and just coats the back of the spoon. Do *not* boil.

3 Pour into 6 individual soufflé dishes or ramekins and cool for at least 30 minutes. Freeze for 3–4 hours until firm. Wrap in cling film and return to the freezer.

4 Serve straight from the freezer, decorated with cherries and peel.

INDEX

Almond peach brûlées 57
Apricot:
    Fresh apricot flan 44
    Sherried apricot trifle 50
Asparagus mousses 7
Aubergine dip 11
Avocado with prawns and smoked
    salmon 12

Beef:
    Beef and olive salad 17
    Cold beef in soured cream 16
    Fillet steak en croûte with
        mushrooms 18
Blackberry ice cream 58

Camembert, deep-fried 15
Chef's salad 39
Chicken:
    Chicken with tarragon sauce 24
    Coronation chicken 25
Chilli potato salad 38
Chocolate:
    Squidgy chocolate mousse
        cake 48
Coffee Bavarian cream 53
Coronation chicken 25
Courgette:
    Iced courgette soup 5
Crab:
    Dressed crab 28
Cream crowdie 49
Cucumber salad 36

Desserts 40–61
Dips 11
Dressed crab 28

Gazpacho 4
Geranium grape sorbet 59

Greek garlic dip 11

Hummus 11

Iced courgette soup 5
Iced orange sabayon 61
Iced tomato and herb soup 6

Lamb:
    Lamb with cucumber and mint
        stuffing 21
    Lamb noisettes in port and red-
        currant sauce 20

Mackerel:
    Spiced grilled mackerel 32
Melon basket, to make a 54
Meringue basket 42
Monkfish and mussel brochettes 30
Mousse:
    Asparagus mousses 7
Mushroom:
    Fillet steak en croûte with
        mushrooms 18
Mussel:
    Monkfish and mussel
        brochettes 30

Orange:
    Iced orange sabayon 61
    Oranges en surprise 60

Papa ghanooye 11
Passion fruit:
    Party passion Pavlova 40
Pasta, prawn and apple salad 35
Pavlova 40
Peach:
    Almond peach brûlées 57
Pineapple:
    Meringue basket 42
Pissaladière 27
Potato:
    Chilli potato salad 38

Prawn:
    Avocado with prawns and smoked
        salmon 12
    Pasta, prawn and apple salad 35
    Prawn and dill tartlets 13

Radicchio and alfalfa salad 37
Raspberry:
    Strawberries with raspberry
        sauce 56
    Summer fruit salad 54

Salade tiède aux lardons 14
Salads 34–9
Sherried apricot trifle 50
Skordalia 11
Smoked salmon:
    Avocado with prawns and smoked
        salmon 12
Soups 4–6
Squidgy chocolate mousse cake 48
Starters 7–15
Strawberry:
    Strawberries with raspberry
        sauce 56
    Strawberry custard flan 45
    Strawberry shortcakes 47
    Summer fruit salad 54

Tali machchli 32
Tarragon sauce, chicken with 24
Tomato:
    Iced tomato and herb soup 6
    Tomato ice with vegetable
        julienne 8
Trifle 50
Turkey paprika with pasta 26

Veal:
    Veal in marsala 22
    Viennese veal escalopes 23
Vegetable dips 11

Waldorf salad 34
Wiener schnitzel 23

GOOD HOUSEKEEPING

...For the life women <u>REALLY</u> lead

Dear Reader,

We do hope you will enjoy your **Good Housekeeping** cookery book and will go on to collect the other titles available from your **BP Service Station.** Each recipe given has been double tested for success by our highly respected and unique resource, the **Good Housekeeping Institute,** so you can try new dishes with complete confidence.

It is that same confidence and trust that makes millions of women read our **Good Housekeeping** magazine each month. Colourful and glossy, it is always brimming over with new and exciting ideas, plus practical advice on a huge range of topics that affect all our everyday lives. No wonder so many people now subscribe to **Good Housekeeping** each month to ensure they don't miss a single copy.

Uniquely for BP customers we are offering a special introductory rate to all new UK subscribers of only £11.20 — a saving of £2 on the current rate! For this amount you will receive a copy of Good Housekeeping by post each month for 12 months.

Credit card holders can order by telephoning 0444 440421 or by post to the address below.

Happy reading!

Publishing Director — Good Housekeeping
Brian Braithwaite

Subscription enquiries and orders with payment to:
Quadrant Subscription Services, FREEPOST, Haywards Heath, West Sussex RH16 3ZA.
Offer closes 31st August 1989.

IMPORTANT: TO QUALIFY FOR YOUR DISCOUNT QUOTE "SAK" IN ALL COMMUNICATIONS.

Published by Ebury Press
Division of The National Magazine Company Ltd
Colquhoun House
27–37 Broadwick Street
London W1V 1FR

The Good Housekeeping Institute is the food and consumer research centre of
Good Housekeeping magazine.
Printed and bound in Italy by New Interlitho, S.p.a., Milan